SCHOOL SHADOW

GUIDELINES

Alex Liau W.M. & Dr. Jed Baker

FUTURE HORIZONS INC.

Arlington, Texas

School Shadow Guidelines

Worldwide marketing and publishing rights, excluding Singapore, guaranteed to and reserved by:

FUTURE HORIZONS INC.

817-277-0727 (local)
817-277-2270 (fax)
email: info@FHautism.com
www.FHautism.com

Originally published by:

Nurture Pods Pte Ltd
314 Thomson Road
Eng Aun Mansion
Singapore 307659

© Nurture Pods Pte Ltd 2013

All rights reserved. No part of this publication may be reproduced, stored in a retrieval system, or transmitted in any form or by any means, electronic, mechanical, photocopying, recording, or otherwise, without the prior permission of the copyright owner.

First Singapore edition published 2013
Future Horizons edition published 2015

Front Cover Design: John Yacio

ISBN-13 978-1-941765-1-11

CONTENTS

ACKNOWLEDGMENTS

The authors wish to thank

Ang Ee Teng and Soh Yong Hao

for their contributions to the development of the *School Shadow Guidelines*.

SCHOOL SHADOW GUIDELINES

THE ROLE OF A
SCHOOL SHADOW

>> The job titles of "School Shadow," "Aide," and "Paraprofessional" are often used interchangeably. Yet, depending on location, these titles may imply some differences in the amount of education required of the individual filling those roles. Although this book uses the term *Shadow*, it does not distinguish it from the other terms. *Shadow* was the title used by Nurture Pods in its programs to support students with autism in schools in Singapore. I consulted with Nurture Pods to help them create this set of guidelines for their staff, who served as *Shadows* for children in their schools.

>> *Shadows* are on the front line of helping students with disabilities. Although they are not responsible for creating many of the academic, social, and behavioral supports for a student, they often have primary responsibility for implementing those strategies during the school day. They serve as a primary safety and support to help a student successfully meet academic and social demands.

>> A team of teachers, behaviorists, consultants, and learning specialists, together with parents, and (perhaps) the student, all create the modifications and adaptations to school demands. However, it is often the school shadow who is asked to help implement many of those modifications, cue new skills, reward particular behaviors, and monitor progress. As the name implies, a shadow may stay close by a student, if needed. The shadow may be the first to recognize when the child needs to refocus or when the child is too frustrated and needs more help, or a break.

>> Although a child may start out as quite dependent on a shadow for help, the ultimate goal is to help the child move to greater independence. Instead of doing the work for the child, the shadow supplies just the right amount of help to allow a child to do the work.

>> Overtime, the shadow hopes to teach the child ways to manage him or herself without being dependent on the shadow. This might include helping the child know that it is okay to ask for help or a

break, or to use visual aids or other reminder systems. These may eventually allow the shadow to do less coaching and cuing. It might also involve creating more natural systems of supports, utilizing peers, rather than relying solely on the shadow for help.

Jed Baker, Ph.D.

PHILOSOPHY

>> We are educators—not disciplinarians. Our job is to help students understand their academic work and learn ways to cope with their challenges.

>> Although some children may engage in challenging behavior willfully, we assume that this behavior is because they do not know a better way. Therefore, we strive to teach them better ways to handle difficult situations.

>> Our effectiveness and trust with the child depends on keeping our negative emotions in check. Rather than give in to the child out of fear, or lose our tempers out of anger, we seek to understand why the child is having difficulty and teach him or her better ways to manage. It can take minutes, hours, days, or sometimes months to learn new ways to cope with challenges.

WORKING IN A TEAM

IT IS CRUCIAL THAT THE TEACHER, YOU, THE CHILD'S FAMILY, AND OTHER RELATED PROFESSIONALS WORK CLOSELY TOGETHER IN ORDER FOR INTEGRATION TO BE SUCCESSFUL (SMITH, 2004)

THERAPIST'S ROLE

> At the start of school, meet with the child's teacher(s) and discuss the child's behavior and needs.

> Describe any visual aids or other supports that the child needs.

> Always ask permission from the teacher before introducing new materials (e.g., a visual aid) for the teacher to use.

> Obtain materials or information on the curriculum or school events so that the child can be better prepared and not have a meltdown. (For example, if surprise tests would trigger a meltdown, ask the teacher to disclose the dates of those tests.)

> Keep a record of the child's performance in school.

>> Always update the communication book in proper English or email the update to the parents by a stipulated time.

>> If there is any important information (e.g., homework or consent forms that need to be signed), telephone or text the parents.

. . . .

PROGRAM MANAGER'S ROLE

> Developing the child's IEP (Individualized Education Plan) with teachers, school personnel, parents, and therapist

> Meeting with school personnel, parents, and therapist for review of child's progress

> Ensuring strategies for the child are up-to-date and relevant

> Monitoring the therapist's conduct and performance

TEACHER'S ROLE

> Developing the child's IEP (Individualized Education Plan) with school personnel, parents, therapists, and other related professionals

> Meeting with school personnel, parents, therapists, and other related professionals for review of the child's progress

> Using encouraging tone and ensuring lots of positive reinforcement (e.g., rewards, encouragement)

> Ensuring that strategies (which have been jointly discussed earlier) are used in the classroom to reinforce the child's performance

CONSISTENCY IS CRUCIAL TO THE CHILD.

SCHOOL PERSONNEL ROLE

> Developing the child's IEP (Individualized Education Plan) with teachers, parents, therapists, and other related professionals

> Meeting with teachers, parents, therapists, and other related professionals for review of the child's progress

> Using an encouraging tone and ensuring lots of positive reinforcement (e.g., rewards, encouragement)

> Possibly modifying curriculum to suit the child's needs

> Arranging accommodation for a child's unique needs (e.g., if the child cannot stand being in a crowd or hearing loud noises, he can stay somewhere quiet during assembly.) This will greatly help the child and aid in alleviating his anxiety

PARENTS' ROLE

> Cooperating with teachers, parents, therapists, and other related professionals

> Reviewing the child's progress with teachers, parents, therapists, and other professionals

> Using encouraging tone and ensuring lots of positive reinforcement at home (e.g., rewards, encouragement)

> Using strategies implemented or recommended by the therapist or program manager (e.g., reading social stories to child on a daily basis and consistently using daily schedules and a visual calendar)

CONSISTENCY IS CRUCIAL TO THE CHILD.

"Our goal is to discover how using visual strategies to support communication can make a difference in each student's life"

Linda Hodgdon, 2001

JOB SCOPE:

PRIMING

THE CHILD

FOR SCHOOL

IF YOU HAVE NOT WORKED WITH THE CHILD BEFORE ENTERING SCHOOL, YOU WILL NEED TO PREPARE HIM FOR SCHOOL. PLEASE NOTE THE FOLLOWING.

ROUTINE OF SCHOOL

>> *Visual schedules* help in daily living skills, academics, and reducing inappropriate behavior. They are particularly helpful to students with autism who have difficulty with language comprehension. Visual schedules make concrete what is abstract and can clearly indicate what had been completed, and what must be done next (Marks, et al., 2003).

>> If possible, obtain the timetable beforehand and do up a visual with color coding.

>> The timetable must be handy and small enough to be carried or placed in the child's pencil case.

>> Use the visuals as prompts for transitions and routines. One schedule will be used for daily lessons and another one used for the week. (*Refer to Appendix B*)

TRANSITIONS

Please take note of the following on your first day working with the child.

TIMETABLE

1. Prepare the color-coded timetable beforehand.

2. The timetable must be handy and small enough to carry or be put in the child's pencil case.

3. With the teacher's approval, place the timetable on a corner of the child's desk for easy reference.

EVENTS

1. Let the child know in advance what is going to happen.

2. Use Social Stories™ or a picture sequence to convey the order of events and what will take place.

3. Preparing the child with the Social Story prior to event may help the child in decreasing his anxiety and improving behavior (Vakil, et al, 2009). *(Refer to Appendix C)*

4. Read a Social Story to the child several times in advance of the event, and then immediately prior to the event.

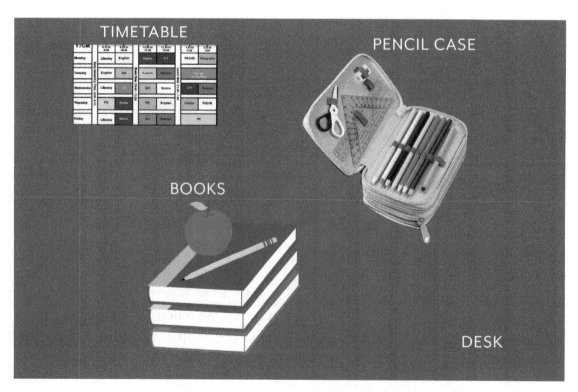

TIMETABLE

PENCIL CASE

BOOKS

DESK

JOB SCOPE:

PROVIDING INSTRUCTIONS

PROVIDE STRUCTURE THROUGH VISUAL SCHEDULES, ROUTINES, AND INSTRUCTIONS.

SHOW THE CHILD THE AVAILABLE VISUAL AIDS RATHER THAN VERBALLY PROMPTING HIM OR HER FOR EACH SET OF INSTRUCTIONS.

NOTE

- Keep the instructions concise

- First, teach the child the visual routine

- You can seek permission from the teacher to pull him aside for a few minutes and go through the visual with him

- Always seek permission from your program manager before phasing-out the visual.

- Allow the child to be as independent as possible (e.g., packing his bag, writing down homework, and buying food)

>> Do this in a non-attention getting manner so as not to disrupt the classroom flow.

>> You can try using pointing or gesturing as a prompt for the child to look at the teacher.

>> If needed, follow up with words like ,"Look at the teacher."

>> If the child misses the instructions, write them on a portable dry erase board. If necessary, repeat instructions or have the child ask his classmate to repeat them.

>> Seat the child in a position of least distraction. Consult with the teacher or your program manager regarding this.

DURING CLASS TIME

EXAMPLE: READING ALOUD WITH THE CLASS

>> If the child is unable to follow, consider using a visual picture sequence of the story to help him understand

>> Ask the child to model after a classmate

>> Provide the child with his own copy of the book (at the teacher's discretion), so that he can review prior to class time and will be primed for listening (Marks, et al., 2003)

>> Let the teacher know that the child is not focused and suggest that he ask the child to turn the pages of the book so that he can feel a sense of involvement

FOR EXAMPLE: DOING MATHEMATICS

>> Provide visual support ("times" table, addition and subtraction table, etc.) First, ask permission from the teacher

>> Children with autism tend to learn better through visuals. Providing visuals may help significantly (Friend 2008; Rao and Gagie 2006)

>> Allow more time for the student to complete the work (Marks et al, 2003)

>> If necessary, take the child aside and explain the assignment one-on-one

DOING OTHER TASKS

>> First, let the child try the task to build independence, but do not let frustration build to the point of outburst. Prompt the child to ask for help and then simplify work for him, if necessary.

>> When the student engages in task refusal, prompt him or her to watch first, ask for help, or ask for a short break (timed at 1-to-2 minutes), and then return to work.

"GOOD TEACHERS UNDERSTAND THAT FOR A CHILD TO LEARN, THE TEACHING STYLE MUST MATCH THE STUDENT'S LEARNING STYLE."

Dr. Temple Grandin
The Way I See It — A Personal Look at Autism & Aspergers's

JOB SCOPE:

TYPES OF REINFORCEMENT

REINFORCEMENTS MAY BE USED IN THE SCHOOL SETTING. WHEN USING REINFORCEMENTS, ESPECIALLY THE ACTIVITY AND TANGIBLE REINFORCEMENTS, BE CAREFUL. THE CHILD MAY LEARN TO AVOID TASKS. IN THIS SITUATION, IT IS IMPORTANT TO CLOSELY OBSERVE THE CHILD'S BEHAVIOR AND LEARN THE REASON FOR TASK AVOIDANCE, INSTEAD OF SIMPLY INCREASING REINFORCEMENT.

>> The type of reinforcement the child gets naturally.

NATURAL REINFORCEMENT

>> The most important natural reinforcement for academic tasks is the joy of the activity itself. Students are more motivated to do work they enjoy and feel they are able to complete. Thus, linking the child's interest to the work (e.g., writing about a favorite topic) or simplifying the work when needed can increase natural motivation to complete tasks.

>> Another natural reinforcement is when behavior leads to a natural reward. For example: a child asks to borrow a book, and his friend replies "Yes!" The child gets a positive answer, which is a natural reinforcement.

SOCIAL REINFORCEMENT

>> This acts as a form of approval for the child.

>> It can be verbal or physical. For example, the child gets a "high-five," eye contact, or verbal approval ("Great job!") after completing an assigned activity.

TOKEN REINFORCEMENT

>> The reward will be given in the form of tokens. The tokens can be accumulated and exchanged for other reinforcement, such as a tangible reward or an activity reinforcement (e.g., reward the child with a sticker for reading well in class; ten stickers can be exchanged for a prize.)

>> You can create an rewards chart to show the child his progress. When the child achieves the desired behaviors (sitting nicely, handing in homework on time, being quiet, etc.), he can receive tokens for those good behaviors.

TANGIBLE REINFORCEMENT

>> These are most useful when tasks are boring and difficult, and result in difficult behavior (e.g., for each page the child completes, he gets a piece of candy or a sticker).

>> ***Tangible reinforcements are not suitable for long-term use.*** The child may get used to the tangible reinforcement, and it will be difficult to wean him or her off the habit of quick gratification.

ACTIVITY REINFORCEMENT

>> Activity reinforcements are best used when tasks are boring or difficult. You may allow the child 5 minutes of reading time after completing school work.

SCHOOL SHADOW GUIDELINES

"If a functional communication system has not been put into place with a student, his only recourse is behavior."

Dr. Temple Grandin
The Way I See It - A Personal Look at Autism & Aspergers's

JOB SCOPE:

BEHAVIOR MANAGEMENT

IN THIS SECTION, WE TOUCH ON HOW TO BETTER MANAGE THE CHILD'S BEHAVIOR AND TANTRUMS USING TOOLS, SUCH AS THE TOKEN ECONOMY AND A POSITIVE BEHAVIORAL SUPPORT PLAN.

Model work for the child before asking him to do it

Use visual supports to explain difficult concepts

Start with easier work to build confidence

DURING DIFFICULT WORK TASKS

Offer to take turns reading or writing to reduce the student's burden

Simplify difficult work by breaking it into smaller tasks

Give the child a choice of how to complete the task (e.g., what he will do first)

Teach the child to cope with frustration by asking for help or a break*

*See "Trying When It's Hard" in Baker, 2008

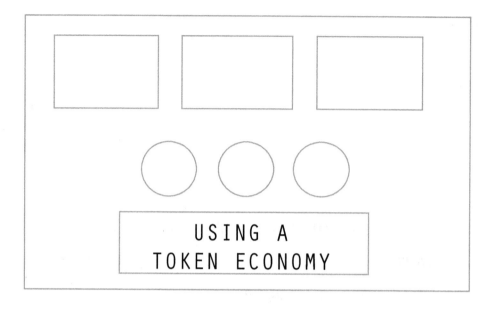

USING A
TOKEN ECONOMY

NOTE

Reward effort, not outcome. Remind the child that he will receive tokens for trying, asking for help, and returning from a break to work, rather than receiving tokens for completing the work correctly. We are trying to build cooperation rather than perfect work completion for a resistant child.

Tailor the commands to the child's needs.

Use a token economy and place it where it is visible to the child.

Try not to use verbal prompts.

Discreetly give the token or reward.

How to manage meltdowns and out-of-control behavior
(Baker, 2008)

STAGE 1: WHEN ANGER BUILDS

>> Use an anger management aid (See **Appendix D**)

>> Show the child how to use the guide

>> Identify the levels of anger and then select a way he can cope

>> When anger or frustration has built to the point that it is difficult to get the child's attention or engage in problem solving, see *How to Manage Meltdowns and Out-of-Control Behavior*

>> Listen to the child's side of the problem

>> Agree with a kernel of truth, even if the child is wrong about some-things (e.g., "You are correct, the child should not have touched your bag. You cannot hit him, but you are right that he should not have touched your bag. ")

>> Apologize when necessary ("I am so sorry that happened.")

>> Collaborate on a better way to get what the student wants. Ask, "What do you want? Let's find the right way to get that."

STAGE 2 :

CHILD STILL RESPONSIVE TO LOGIC

CALM HIM DOWN

SCHOOL SHADOW GUIDELINES

STAGE 3 :

CHILD OUT OF CONTROL AND NOT LISTENING

↓

DISTRACTION ······➤

NOTE

Consider novel items, special interests, or sensory activities to distract and calm the child

➤➤ *Novel items* are things the child has never seen that might interest him, such as a coin that might be valuable, an interesting picture, or a noise outside the room.

➤➤ *Special interests* might include the child's favorite story book or collectible that you keep on hand for a distraction.

➤➤ *Sensory activities* might include going for a walk outside, listening to music, or a calming touch on the shoulders for children who can tolerate being touched.

❧ Distraction is a temporary crisis tool.

❧ We do not want to get into the habit of distracting a child so that he can avoid work.

❧ When they are trying to avoid work, it is best to simplify and shorten the work before taking a break, rather than engaging in distraction.

SCHOOL SHADOW GUIDELINES

STAGE 4: DEALING WITH RECURRING PROBLEMS

>> When the same problem behaviors keep occurring, we need to keep track of the circumstances in which the problems occur. In a written diary, or using certain apps (such as the No More Meltdown app), we can keep track of the triggers (also called antecedents), behaviors, and consequences of each instance of the problem behavior. (See ABC chart in Appendix E).

>> Review with your program manager how to fill out the ABC sheets or use an app to keep track of the behavior. With your manager, identify the common triggers that lead to behavioral problem and create a prevention plan based on the triggering events (see guide to creating prevention plan from Baker, 2008, shown in Appendix E).

» CREATING A POSITIVE BEHAVIORAL SUPPORT PLAN

(From *No More Meltdowns*, Baker 2008)

IN THIS SECTION, WE LEARN HOW TO CHANGE THE TRIGGERS OR TEACH SKILLS TO DEAL WITH TRIGGERS. HOW CAN WE CHANGE THE TRIGGER TO MAKE IT LESS LIKELY THAT THE CHALLENGING BEHAVIOR WILL OCCUR? WHAT ALTERNATIVE SKILLS CAN WE TEACH THE CHILD TO BETTER COPE WITH THE SITUATIONS THAT TRIGGER PROBLEM BEHAVIORS OR MELTDOWNS? WE WILL ALSO BRIEFLY TOUCH ON REWARD AND LOSS SYSTEMS.

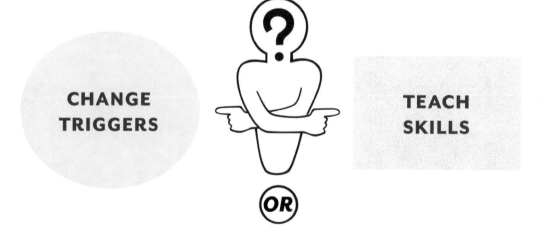

CHANGE THE TRIGGERS

SENSORY STIMULATION

- Alter the noise, light, smell, taste, or touch sensation in the situation. Some children may need quieter environments in which to work.

- Certain individuals find fluorescent lighting to be distracting, and they function better with incandescent or LED lighting.

- Some children find certain textures of foods and specific odors offensive, or they cannot tolerate the feel of certain types of clothing.

- In contrast, other children may crave certain types of sensation, getting bored easily unless there are high levels of stimulation.

TIMING OF SITUATION

- If a child is excessively hungry, tired, or sick, wait until he is fed, rested, and well before asking him to confront a challenging task.

TASK DIFFICULTY

- Make a challenging task easier or shorter in duration.

VISUAL SUPPORTS

- Use pictures or text to increase understanding, or remind students of the steps involved in completing a task.

- Examples include: posters or cue cards that depict rules, or graphic organizers that display information to increase comprehension and recall of stories or information.

- Schedules and timers can be used to help students wait patiently.

SCHOOL SHADOW GUIDELINES

TEACH SKILLS

TRIGGERING SITUATION		PROBLEM BEHAVIOR		ALTERNATIVE SKILLS

1 DEMANDS

Difficult work, chores, sensory challenges, new situations, or social demands. » Avoidance or refusal to participate. » Ask for help.

Imitate others doing the task.

Negotiate how much to do or how to alter a challenging task. *(See Chapter 7)*

2 WAITING

Being denied some activity or object, or having to wait a long time. » Demands, tantrums, or retaliation. » Learn the "invisible pay-off" of waiting or accepting "no."

Learning that others will be happy and give you something later if you can wait. *(See Chapter 8)*

TRIGGERING SITUATION		PROBLEM BEHAVIOR		ALTERNATIVE SKILLS

3 THREATS TO SELF-IMAGE

Teasing, criticism, losing a game, or making mistakes.

>>

Taking it personally as a negative judgment about oneself and one's abilities.

>>

Learn not to perceive these events as judgment about one's own ability or character, but instead see them as a reflection of the other person's issues, or as an opportunity to learn more. (See Chapter 9).

4 UNMET WISHES FOR ATTENTION

Wanting to play or interact with others. Jealousy of others. Fear of being alone.

>>

Annoying others to get them to interact. Complaining that others get more attention. Clinging to others.

>>

Learn effective ways to initiate play. Understand that one is valued even when not getting attention. Learn to self-soothe rather than depend on others (see Chapter 10)

SCHOOL SHADOW GUIDELINES

REWARDS AND LOSS SYSTEMS

THIS REFERS TO REWARDING POSITIVE ALTERNATIVE SKILLS AND SOMETIMES USING A LOSS OF PRIVILEGE FOR ENGAGING IN DISRUPTIVE BEHAVIORS.

Rewards may include praise; material rewards such as access to a toy, special food, or favored games; or point systems that add up to larger rewards, such as buying a new toy or going on a special outing.

Try to avoid taking away privileges, such as TV, computer time, or grounding the child. Losing privileges or rewards should be used only if:

» The triggering situation has been modified

» The child has been taught a better way to deal with the situation

» The child was reminded to engage in the positive behavior

» The child chose the disruptive behavior

JOB SCOPE:

SOCIAL SKILLS MANAGEMENT

YOUR ROLE WILL BE TO PRIME, COACH, AND REVIEW WITH YOUR PROGRAM MANAGER THE SOCIAL SKILLS GOALS THAT WERE PREVIOUSLY SET. YOU WILL ALSO NEED TO FACILITATE SOCIAL INTERACTION AND HELP THE CHILD TO REACT APPROPRIATELY IN SOCIAL SITUATIONS THAT CAN OCCUR AT ANY TIME.

PRIME	⸱⸱⸱⸱⸱⸱▸	COACH	⸱⸱⸱⸱⸱⸱▸	REVIEW

Prime skills before they are needed (e.g., if the child is working on respecting others' physical space, we might remind him to keep an arm's length away just prior to getting in line, or in any situation where he is close to others).

Coach the skill as it is needed (e.g., "You're getting too close, keep an arm's length away.")

Review For example, after social events ask, "Were you able to respect the space of others?"

>> Coach the child to respond to others

>> Greet peers and teachers

>> Respect others' space and belongings

>> Compromise in group activities

>> Ask peers for help as needed

>> Coach the child and peers to interact directly with each other, rather than talking through you as a mediator

>> Kluth (2004) suggests that the child's interests be taken into consideration during the activity. Use visual supports to enhance the child's willingness to participate (Lantz, et al, 2004)

>> Allow the child to demonstrate his strengths in front of peers

EXAMPLE 1: DURING PE

The class is having PE, and the child is particularly good at soccer. Ask the teacher to allow the child to demonstrate to his peers how to play soccer.

EXAMPLE 2: IN CLASS

The class is doing some math, and his classmate does not know how to do a particular question. Encourage the child to assist his classmate.

SCHOOL SHADOW GUIDELINES

>> When pairing your child with another student, you may want to train the other student to be sensitive to the challenges of your child. If you are going to speak to others about your child, first ask permission from the parents and the program manager about what you will say to the child's peers.

You can do the following:

Discuss how the child is the same as everyone else in some ways and different in other ways

>> Discuss the child's specific challenges. Explain that due to those challenges, he may sometimes do things that bother others, but it is not intentional.

>> For example, John is a part of this class, just the same as everyone else. He takes the same subjects and buys food during recess just like the other pupils in his school.

>> Sometimes, however, John may be a bit loud when reading his favorite storybook, or he may shout at his teachers. These behaviors are not intentional, as John does not understand that these behaviors can upset others. You are his classmate, so you may remind him gently and give him some space and time to improve. John may then imitate you when you demonstrate exemplary behavior.

Include a discussion of the child's talents and liken his profile of strengths and challenges to other famous talented individuals. (e.g., Albert Einstein, Bill Gates, and others who may have had social challenges despite good intellectual abilities in other areas).

NOTE

- Always seek permission from the teacher before pairing a child with peers
- Consider peers with good social and communication skills and those who show interest in helping others

JOB SCOPE:

SEQUENCE OF FADING

> Start off with enough prompting to ensure success and then lessen the intensity of prompts over time to see if the child can behave more independently (Leach, 2010).

> In the first 3 months of school shadow, we recommend that you sit beside or within arm's length of the child (if he will tolerate your proximity).

> When a child's behavior is more stable, inform your program manager. You may then sit further away from the child (perhaps moving to the back of the classroom, where you will still be able to observe the child.

> After the 3 months, depending on the child, there may be a change in timing or distance. Consult with your program manager before implementing a change.

I am first and foremost a child.

I have autism.

I am not primarily "autistic."

Ellen Notbohm, 2005. *Ten Things Every Child with Autism Wishes You Knew*

JOB SCOPE:

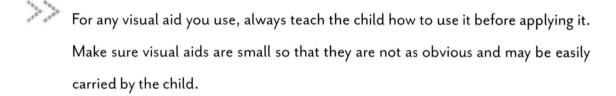

IMPORTANT POINTS

>> For any visual aid you use, always teach the child how to use it before applying it. Make sure visual aids are small so that they are not as obvious and may be easily carried by the child.

>> Give instructions clearly and simply.

>> Be firm and consistent.

>> Redirect tantrums to the appropriate replacement skill (e.g., ask for help or a break). If the tantrum is occurring to escape work, then have the child do a smaller amount of work. Simplify the work rather than allowing the child to avoid all work. If tantrum is not intended to avoid work, then first try to distract the child (see section 5: How to Manage Meltdowns).

>> In the event that the child's behavior is disrupting the class, and he is unable to calm, take the child out of class and let him calm down.

CASE STUDIES

THE MOST IMPORTANT PART IS TO KNOW WHICH STRATEGIES TO APPLY AND WHAT VISUALS TO USE FOR THE ISSUES YOUR CHILD IS FACING. WE WILL EXAMINE 3 CASE STUDIES AND SUGGEST WAYS TO ADDRESS THE ISSUES THAT ARISE.

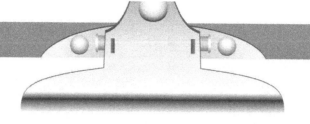

CASE STUDY 1

Child: Javier

Issues: Unable to keep up with the class. Disrupts the class by refusing to change to the next activity because he has not finished his work.

SUGGESTIONS

>> Create a ***visual schedule*** for Javier. The class timetable can be color coded. Use gestural prompting (e.g., point to a timetable) and use verbal prompting the first couple of times you implement this strategy. As the time to stop is approaching, remind him that if he leaves his work unfinished, he will still be able to return to it later so he will not miss the instructions for the next activity. Javier may also get a point on his behavior/rewards chart.

>> ***Create a folder*** for Javier that says "Unfinished Work". Teach Javier to put his unfinished work into the folder. Create a Social Story to explain that he can finish his work later. Also, remind him that if he moves on, he will not miss the instructions for the next assignment. He also will not disrupt the class this way. If necessary, use verbal prompting for the first few tries.

>> Reinforce this behavior by providing positive feedback, or use the ***token economy***.

>> You can create a ***Social Story***™ using the 10-step manual and have it read to him everyday, before school, or at night.

Case Study 2

Child: Ed

Issues: Shouts at his peers when one of them gets a turn first.

Unable to accept "No" when peers will not give him something he wants (e.g., when asking to borrow a book from a friend).

Aim: Alter situations to avoid triggering an upset (e.g., not going first, being denied an object he wants) and teach him to recognize the triggers and better mange those situations.

SUGGESTIONS

ACCEPTING "NO"

>> Change the trigger: Use **visual supports** to show Ed what is his and what is not his. Explain that he can have what is his, but he cannot always have what is not his.

>> Use a **schedule** to show Ed when he can have some of the things he wants. Use a timer to help him take turns in class.

>> Teach him how to accept "no" or "wait." Explain that if he stays calm, Ed has a higher chance of getting what he wants because others will be happy.

>> Before he asks a peer for something, remind Ed that if they say no, he will still be able to have item X or Y (an alternative item which acts as an reward for being able to calmly accept "No").

>> Create a **token economy by** explaining to Ed that he will get tokens every time he accepts "No" calmly. Tokens then can be exchanged for rewards.

>> Create a personalized **Social Story** for Ed using the 10-step manual and have it read to him everyday.

NOT GOING FIRST

>> Change the trigger: Let Ed have the first turn when you play a game, but remind him him that the next time his friend will go first. It will be easier to learn to wait for his turn if we let him be first when we begin teaching him this.

>> Teach how and why to let others go first. Explain that others will like him more and want to play if he can let them go first. Ed will WIN A FRIEND when he lets others go first.

>> You can create a personalized **Social Story** using the 10-step manual and have it read to Ed every day.

CASE STUDY 3

Child: Sam

Issues: Whenever the class laughs, Sam thinks everyone is making fun of him. He gets angry and lashes out

Aim: To get Sam to better understand his classmates' perspectives and to manage his anger

SUGGESTIONS

USE PICTURE BOOKS

Use picture books to show Sam what people are thinking when they are laughing. Explain that they are usually thinking of something funny, not laughing at him.

TOKEN ECONOMY

Use a **token economy** and reward Sam when he is showing the targeted behavior (e.g., how to respond when friends laugh). When he is not responding appropriately, do not take away the token. Instead, wait longer before rewarding Sam again. Also only reward Sam when he shows the targeted behavior.

SOCIAL STORY

Develop a **Social Story** based on the 10-step manual and have it read to Sam everyday before school, or at night.

TEACH

Teach Sam how to respond to others laughter. He might ask, "Are you laughing at me?"

>> If they say no, then remember its not about you.

>> If they say yes, then ask them to stop. If they do not stop, tell the teacher.

Remember, do not lose your temper at them because then you get in trouble.

ANGER MANAGEMENT AID

Develop an **anger management guide** together with Sam. Discuss with Sam the levels of anger he experiences and suggest how he may handle it. Make a small copy for him to refer to in school.

SCHOOL SHADOW GUIDELINES

REFERENCES

Baker, J. *No More Meltdowns, Positive Strategies for Managing and Preventing Out-of-Control Behavior.* Arlington, TX: Future Horizons, 2008.

Friend, M. & W. D. Bursuck. *Including Students with Special Needs: A Practical Guide for Classroom Teachers.* Upper Saddle River, NJ: Pearson, 2009.

Goodman, G. & C. M. Williams. "Interventions for Increasing the Academic Engagement of Students with Autism Spectrum Disorders in Inclusive Classrooms." Teaching Exceptional Children, 39(6), 53-61, 2007.

Kluth, P. "Autism, Autobiography and Adaptations." Teaching Exceptional Children, 6(4), 42–47, 2004.

Lantz, J. F., J. M. Nelson, & R. L. Loftin. "Guiding Children with Autism in Play: Applying the Integrated Play Group Model in School Settings." Exceptional Children, 37(2), I8–I14, 2004

Leach, D. *Bringing ABA into Your Inclusive Classroom: A Guide to Improving Outcomes for Students With Autism Spectrum Disorders.* (1st ed.) Baltimore: Paul H Brookes Publishing Co., 2010.

Marks, S. U-, J. Shaw-Hegwer, C. Schrader, T. Longaker, I. Peters, E. Powers, et al. "Instructional Management Tips for Teachers of Students with Autism Spectrum Disorder (ASD)." Teaching Exceptional Children. 35, 50-55, 2003.

Rao, S. M., & B. Gagie. "Learning Through Seeing and Doing. Visual Supports of Children with Autism." Teaching Exceptional Children, 38(6), 26–33, 2006.

Reinhartsen, D. B., A. N. Garfinkle, and M. Wolery. "Engagement with Toys in Two-Year Old Children with Autism: Teacher Selection versus Child Choice," Journal of the Association for Persons with Severe Handicaps, 27, 175-178, 2002.

Smith, D. D. *Introduction to Special Education: Teaching in an Age of Opportunity.* Boston, MA: Allyn & Bacon, 2004.

Vakil, S., E. Welton, B. O'Connor, L. S. Kline. "Inclusion Means Everyone! The Role of the Early Childhood Educator when Including Young Children with Autism in the Classroom," Early Childhood Education Journal, 36, 321-326, 2008.

APPENDIX A

TOKEN ECONOMY

What ?

>> A token economy is a reward system for managing children's behavior.

>> Every time a child exhibits the desired behavior, he earns a token. When he has collected an agreed number of tokens, he may exchange those tokens for a reward

Guidelines

>> In creating a token economy, you should bear in mind the functioning level of a child.

>> Preferably, you should start with only 3 targeted behaviors (e.g., sitting, quiet, hands down)

>> With a higher-functioning child, more targeted behaviors can be used.

>> If you are not sure what the child's functioning level is, please consult with your program managers before creating the materials.

SAMPLE TOKEN ECNONOMY

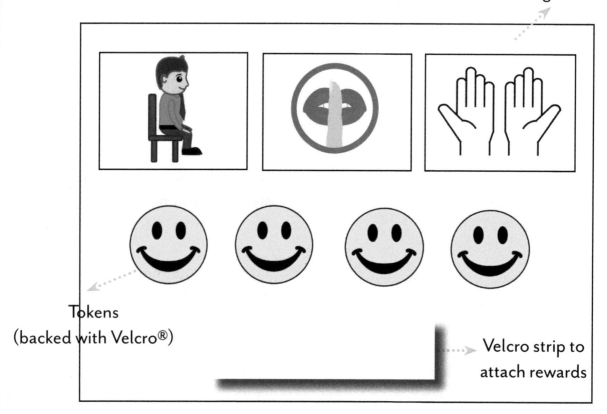

Targeted Behaviors

Tokens
(backed with Velcro®)

Velcro strip to
attach rewards

PROCESS OF USING TOKEN ECONOMY

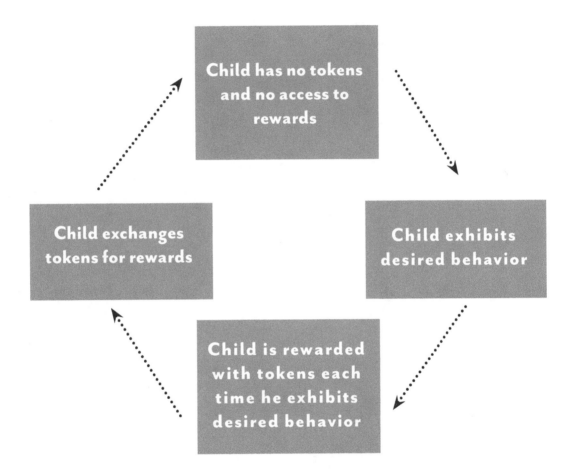

VISUAL SCHEDULES

WHAT?

>> Visual schedules are primarily used to help children organize their daily activities as well as increase their understanding of the sequence of activities (e.g., personal hygiene, breakfast, bus, class, recess, class, lunch, bus, play, etc.).

>> Letting children with autism know what is happening around them helps to reduce the anxiety and stress that come with transitions (e.g., changing from one activity to another).

>> There are 3 types of visual schedules:

- Visual Calendars

- Visual Activity / Class Schedule

- Visual Routine

>> Their roles are similar but the content varies from general to specific.

General Event to Specific Tasks

VISUAL CALENDAR	VISUAL ACTIVITY / CLASS SCHEDULE	VISUAL ROUTINE

» A visual *calendar* is used to mark significant or stressful days for the child (e.g., field trip, doctor's visit, or birthday) and is usually presented in month format.

NOVEMBER 2015						
SUNDAY	MONDAY	TUESDAY	WEDNESDAY	THURSDAY	FRIDAY	SATURDAY
1	2	3	4	5	6	7
8	9	10	11	12	13	14
15	16	17	18	19	20	21
22	23	24	25	26	27	28
29	30	1	2	3	4	5

>> A visual *schedule* shows specific activities for the a day or a week.

DAILY SCHEDULE

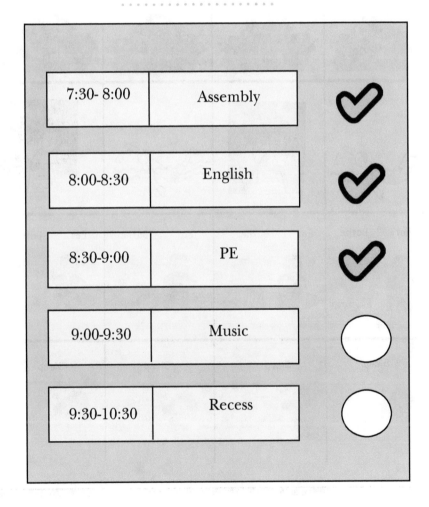

7:30- 8:00	Assembly	✓
8:00-8:30	English	✓
8:30-9:00	PE	✓
9:00-9:30	Music	◯
9:30-10:30	Recess	◯

WEEKLY SCHEDULE

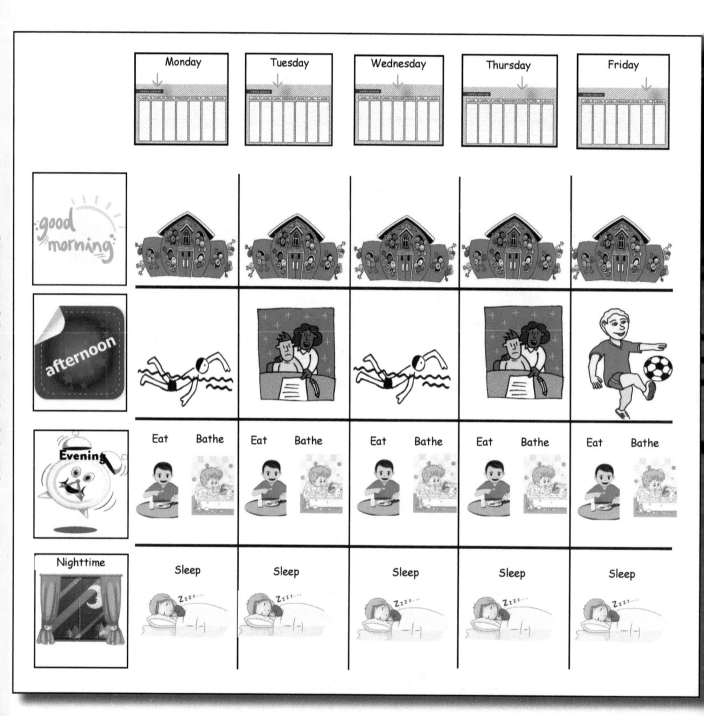

A visual *routine* aims to inform, teach, and prompt a child on specific tasks or actions (e.g., going to the toilet or washing hands).

DAILY ROUTINE

My Morning Routine

Today is | Monday

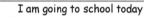
I am going to school today

| Wake up | Make bed | Brush teeth | Shower |

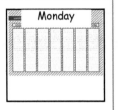   

| Get dressed | Eat breakfast | School bag | School bus |

SPECIFIC TASK ROUTINE

DOING WORK

Write name	Write Answer	Color	Give to Teacher

DURING EXAMS OR TESTS

1) Receive Paper

2) Wait for the teacher to give instructions and say "Begin!"

3) Write my name

4) Read every question carefully

5) If I do not know how to do a question, I move on and go back when I have

finished my paper.

6) After all questions are done, check the paper.

7) When the teacher says "Stop!" stop writing and put my test paper down

APPENDIX C

SOCIAL STORY™

WHAT ?

>> Social stories are simple stories that teach children with autism appropriate behavior and social skills.

>> A Social Story describes a situation where an individual has difficulty and it tells what to expect from other people in that situation and what is expected from the individual.

>> You can use Social Stories to address a child's difficult behaviors.

GUIDELINES

>> The 10 criteria used in this manual are based on *The New Social Stories™ Book Revised and Expanded 10th Anniversary Edition* (Carol Gray, 2010). Use that book with *School Shadow Guidelines* to better understand what Social Stories are and how to use them effectively.

>> Please use this manual at your own discretion. This is by no means a "bible" that you should stick to at all cost. Every child is unique. Therefore, the content of a Social Story may differ for each child.

SCHOOL SHADOW GUIDELINES

STEP ONE: GOAL

THE GOAL: Help Billy understand why he has to wear a seat belt when he rides the school bus.

....

STEP TWO: DISCOVERY

SOURCES OF INFORMATION

PARENTS

>> When Billy travels with his parents on city buses, seat belts are not required.

>> Twice, Billy's mother accompanied him on the school bus, and he could wear his seat belt throughout the journey. However, his parents cannot always accompany him.

>> Whenever Billy has a meltdown (for other issues), his parents will give Billy his favorite soft toy, Beany the Bear. Touching the fur on Beany's ears calms Billy.

BUS DRIVER OR PARAPROFESSIONAL

>> The bus driver or paraprofessional has difficulty getting Billy to put on his seat belt when he takes the bus to school and back home.

>> Billy's school district requires students to wear seat belts on school buses.

THERAPIST   >>   Positive reinforcement does not last long enough to keep Billy in his seat and wearing with his seat belt.

FRIENDS   >>   Friends of his age can put on their seat belts when they board the bus and sometimes laugh at Billy for being "naughty."

CAREGIVER   >>   Billy's main caregivers are his parents.

BILLY   >>   Billy resists attempts to put on the seat belt but cannot verbalize his reason. He simply says "I don't like, I don't like, I don't want, I don't want," and he keeps pulling the seat belt away from his chest. Perhaps, Billy does not like the seat belt against his body.

NOTE

✦   This is a list of words you should NOT use in a Social Story™

PROHIBITED VOCABULARY

1. Should / Shouldn't
2. Supposed to
3. Must / Mustn't
4. Ought / Ought to know better
5. It's really (bad / naughty / inappropriate) to...
6. Caution: Can

TYPES OF INFORMATION TO SHARE

OBJECTIVE
....
INFORMATION

>> Billy does not like to put on the seat belt when he takes the school bus.

>> For safety, it is important to wear a seat belt.

>> The school district requires students to wear seat belts when riding the school bus.

>> His friends wear seat belts when riding the bus.

COGNITIVE
....
PROCESS

>> He can bring his toy bear on the bus to calm himself.

>> Remind Billy of times when he successfully wore his seat belt when riding the bus.

TEMPORAL
....
CONNECTIONS

>> Twice, Billy wore his seat belt on the bus, but on both occasions, Billy's mother rode with him.

>> He will need to take the school bus every day for at least the next year (until he finishes preschool).

STEP THREE: "SIX QUESTION" GUIDE STORY

WHO

>> Billy & Bus Driver or Paraprofessional

WHERE

>> On the school bus

WHEN

>> Every day when he goes to school and when he comes home.

WHAT

>> Billy needs to wear his seat belt when he takes the bus, but he does not like to wear it.

>> Billy can use Beany, his favorite toy bear to calm.

>> Wearing a seat belt is a school rule, and it is for Billy's safety.

>> Billy needs to continue taking the school bus for the next year, until he finishes preschool.

HOW

>> Billy resists putting on his seat belt, and positive reinforcement is not enough to motivate him to wear it.

WHY

>> Perhaps Billy resists wearing his seat belt because he does not like it strapped across his chest.

SCHOOL SHADOW GUIDELINES

STEP FOUR: FORMAT

AGE
. . . .
ABILITY

>> Billy is 5 years old, and started preschool this year. His receptive linguistic ability is much better than his expressive linguistic ability. He is able to understand simple sentences with subject-verb-object but has difficulty expressing himself.

>> Billy's attention span is rather short.

>> Keep the story short and simple so that it can keep Billy's attention.

REPETITION
. . . .
RHYME

>> Avoid repetition because Billy's attention span is quite short.

>> Keep sentences short and to the point.

>> Rhyme might capture Billy's attention and make the story fun for him.

ILLUSTRATIONS
. . . .

>> Use simple illustrations that are not too overwhelming. Illustrations should also not be mixed in the text (perhaps put at the side) to make it easier for Billy to follow.

>> The text should be large enough to be easily read by Billy.

SCHOOL SHADOW GUIDELINES

STEP FIVE: NINE MAKES IT MINE

PREFERENCE

He likes space and does not like to be kept in a confined area.

EXPERIENCE

Previously, Billy rode the school bus with his mother and wore his seat belt throughout the journey.

TAILORING TO THE CHILD'S ...

TALENT

Billy can sing quite well and likes to sing "Twinkle, Twinkle, Little Star" when he is in a good mood. We can try to turn the story into a song!

INTEREST

He likes his toy bear, Beany, very much, and it calms him when he is experiencing a meltdown.

RELATIONSHIPS

Billy is very close to his mother but does not have any close friends on the bus.

STEP SIX: SEVEN TYPES OF QUESTIONS

Description	>>	I take the school bus to school and back home every day.
	>>	Everyone wears seat belts on the bus.
	>>	The seat belt keeps me safe.

| Perspective | >> | Mommy will be happy if I wear my seat belt. |

| Coach Child | >> | I will try to wear the seat belt on the bus. |

| Coach team | >> | The paraprofessional will help me to put on my seat belt. |

| Self-coaching | >> | I can touch Beany's ears when I wear my seat belt. |

| Affirmative | >> | It is good to wear the seat belt. |
| | >> | I have worn my seat belt before, and I can do it again! |

| Partial | | |

STEP SEVEN: FIVE FACTORS DEFINE VOICE & VOCABULARY

PATIENT AND REASSURING TONE IN STORY INCLUDING...

1st or 3rd person perspective	>> Ensure that ALL sentences do not contain you / your / yours. For example, *I take the school bus to school and back home every day. Everyone wears his seat belt on the bus.*
Positive and patient tone	>> Ensure that first person voice is not used to describe the child's negative behavior. >> Include affirmative sentences! For example, *Mommy will be angry if I don't wear the seat belt.* ✗ *Sometimes, children do not want to put on their seatbelts. This is dangerous. If I put on my seat belt, mommy will be happy!* ✓
Past, present and future	>> Extrapolating a past event to future: Past event: *I have worn my seat belt before and I will do it again!* Future event: *"I will try to wear my seat belt on the bus."*
Literal accuracy	>> Ensure that the sentences are in the clearest language, without requiring the child to read between the lines. For example, *"the seat belt keeps me safe."*
Accurate and comfortable vocabulary	>> Use positive language: Instead of, *"Mommy will be angry if I don't wear the seat belt."* ✗ Say, *"if I put on my seat belt, mommy will be happy!"* ✓ >> Choose of verbs that should not be misinterpreted: Instead of, *"Everyone has a seat belt on the bus."* ✗ Say, *"Everyone wears a seat belt on the bus."* ✓

SCHOOL SHADOW GUIDELINES

Now, you have an edited table of sentences to use in your Social Story™!

Note: not all boxes are filled in, but that is okay.

Description	>>	I take the bus to school and back home every day.
	>>	Everyone has a seat belt on the bus.
	>>	The seat belt keeps me safe.
Perspective	>>	Sometimes, children do not want to put on their seat belts. This is dangerous.
Coach Child	>>	I will try to wear the seat belt on the bus.
Coach team	>>	The bus driver or paraprofessional will help me put on my seat belt.
Self-coaching	>>	I can touch Beany's ears when I put on my seat belt.
Affirmative	>>	It is good to wear my seat belt.
	>>	I have worn my seatbelt before, and I will do it again!
	>>	If I wear on my seat belt, mommy will be happy!
Partial		

STEP EIGHT: THREE PARTS AND A TITLE

IN THIS STORY, I HAVE MADE IT TO THE TUNE OF TWINKLE, TWINKLE, LITTLE STAR. LASTLY, ADD IN A TITLE!

WEARING MY SEAT BELT

I take school bus every day.

Seat belt keeps me very safe.

I will try to wear seat belt.

Mommy will be very proud.

I have Beany here with me.

Wearing a seat belt can make me happy!

SCHOOL SHADOW GUIDELINES

STEP NINE: A "GR-8" FORMULA

USING THE SOCIAL STORY™ (OR SONG) ABOVE, CHECK THAT YOUR STORY DESCRIBES MORE THAN IT DIRECTS.

Number of descriptive sentences + perspective sentences + affirmative sentences = number of DESCRIPTIVE sentences. *Descriptive sentences are shown in red in the example below.*

Number of sentences that coach child + coach team + self-coaching = number of COACHING sentences. *Coaching sentences are shown in blue in the example below.*

Social Stories™ should always include at least twice as many **Descriptive** sentences as **Coaching** sentences.

In the example on the previous page, we have four **Descriptive** sentences and two **Coaching** sentences:

I take school bus every day.	(Descriptive)
Seat belt keeps me very safe.	(Descriptive)
I will try to wear my seat belt.	(Coaching)
Mommy will be very proud.	(Descriptive)
I have Beany here with me.	(Coaching)
Wearing a seat belt can make me happy.	(Descriptive)

DOORS

There are doors everywhere.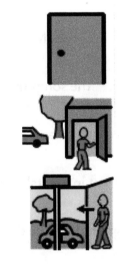

Doors are for going in.

Doors are for going out.

I only touch doors when I need to go in or out.

I go through a door and hold my hands.

I can control myself!

HIGHER LEVEL SOCIAL STORY™

TALKING AND LISTENING

(Insert child's photo)

I am Mary Wilson. My favorite singers are Carrie Underwood, Miranda Lambert, and Brad Paisley. I like to listen to the songs they sing. Sometimes, I will tell my friends about them and play the songs on my phone for them. However,

everyone shares different interests! All of us like different things. It is normal. Sometimes, my friends might not tell me directly that they are not interested in what I say. They might stop answering me or start looking around at other things. When that happens, it might be a good time to stop talking and let my friends have a turn. I can ask my friends "What do you want to talk about?" I can try to listen to my friends talk about about the things that they like. We can learn more about each other. When they ask me about the things I like, I feel happy. When I ask my friends about the things they like, they might be happy too. It is polite for everyone to take turns talking about the things they like. I can be a good listener!

APPENDIX D

ANGER MANAGEMENT AID

WHAT ?

>> The goal of anger management is to reduce negative feelings.

>> The more a child calmly expresses anger, the less likely he will have an angry outburst.

>> You can use the anger management aid to help the child identify his levels of anger and learn to better manage it.

GUIDELINES

>> Sit down with the child and discuss the levels of anger that he experiences.

>> Discuss and suggest the steps he can take to manage the different levels of anger

>> Also, observe the child during his tantrums and make notes of what triggers them.

Examples

Solutions

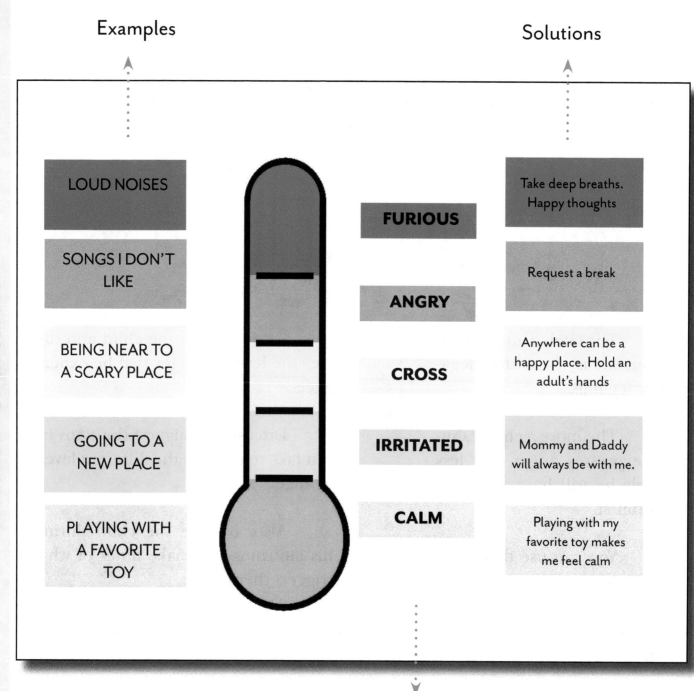

LOUD NOISES

SONGS I DON'T LIKE

BEING NEAR TO A SCARY PLACE

GOING TO A NEW PLACE

PLAYING WITH A FAVORITE TOY

FURIOUS

ANGRY

CROSS

IRRITATED

CALM

Take deep breaths. Happy thoughts

Request a break

Anywhere can be a happy place. Hold an adult's hands

Mommy and Daddy will always be with me.

Playing with my favorite toy makes me feel calm

Emotions
You can use graphics as well, such as photos, cli-part, or illustrations.

ANGER MANAGEMENT AID SAMPLE

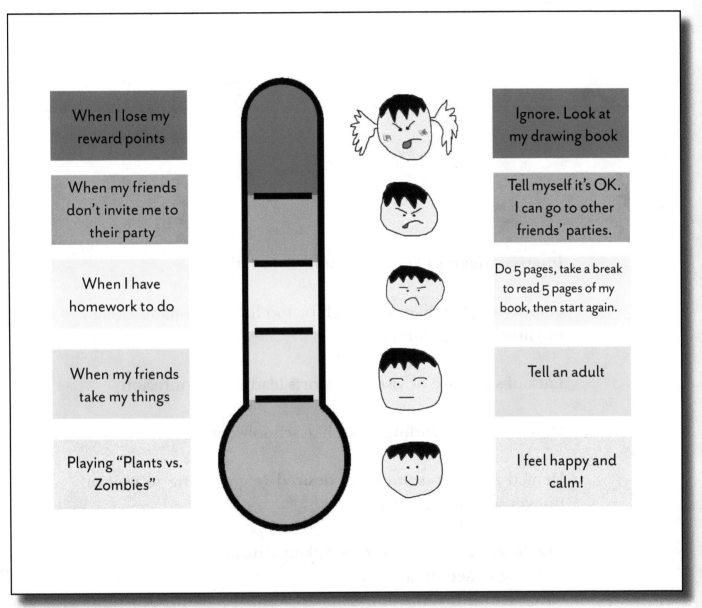

When I lose my reward points

When my friends don't invite me to their party

When I have homework to do

When my friends take my things

Playing "Plants vs. Zombies"

Ignore. Look at my drawing book

Tell myself it's OK. I can go to other friends' parties.

Do 5 pages, take a break to read 5 pages of my book, then start again.

Tell an adult

I feel happy and calm!

> APPENDIX E

ABC ANALYSIS

Antecedent - **B**ehavior - **C**onsequence

ANTECEDENTS/TRIGGERS MAY INCLUDE:

>> Internal triggers like illness, hunger or fatigue

>> Sensory triggers like too much or too little stimulation (e.g., too much noise, boredom)

>> Lack of structure or visual supports leading to confusion

>> Difficult or demanding tasks, like schoolwork

>> Denied access to something desired (e.g., having to wait or not get something desired)

>> Threat to self-esteem, such as making a mistake, losing a game, or being teased or criticized

>> Unmet needs for attention (e.g., being ignored or trying to be the center of attention)

Observer Name: _____ Student Observed:_____

Date of Observation:_____

Antecedent		Behavior	Consequence	
Teacher	Peers	Student	Teacher	Peers

SCHOOL SHADOW GUIDELINES

CPSIA information can be obtained
at www.ICGtesting.com
Printed in the USA
JSHW020343260922
30917JS00001B/1